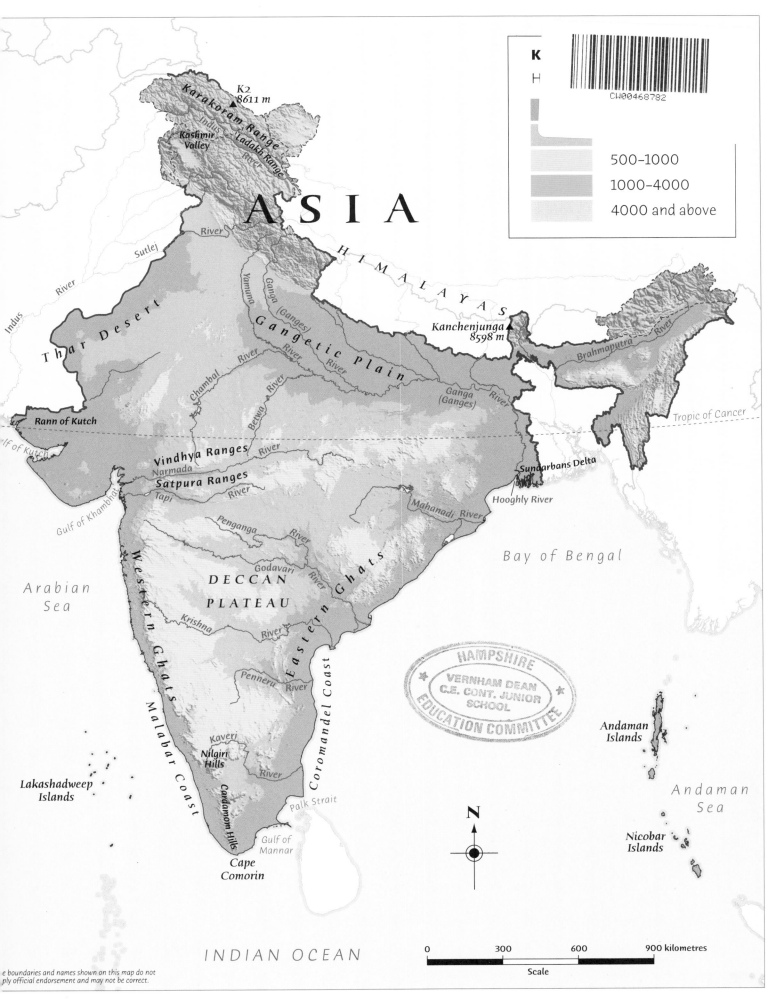

ASIA

K2
8611 m

Karakoram Range

Kashmir
Valley

Ladakh Range

Indus River

HIMALAYAS

Sutlej River

Indus River

Thar Desert

Yamuna

Ganga

Gangetic Plain

Kanchenjunga
8598 m

Brahmaputra River

Chambal River

River

Ganga
(Ganges)

River

Tropic of Cancer

Rann of Kutch

Betwa River

Vindhya Ranges

Gulf of Kutch

Narmada

Satpura Ranges

River

Tapi

Gulf of Khambhat

Penganga

River

Mahanadi River

Sundarbans Delta

Hooghly River

Arabian
Sea

Godavari River

DECCAN
PLATEAU

Eastern Ghats

Bay of Bengal

Western Ghats

Krishna

River

Penneru River

Coromandel Coast

Malabar Coast

Kaveri

Nilgiri
Hills

River

Andaman
Islands

Lakashadweep
Islands

Cardamom Hills

Palk Strait

Gulf of
Mannar

Andaman
Sea

Nicobar
Islands

Cape
Comorin

N

INDIAN OCEAN

0   300   600   900 kilometres

Scale

CW00468782

K

H

500–1000

1000–4000

4000 and above

HAMPSHIRE
VERNHAM DEAN
C.E. CONT. JUNIOR
SCHOOL
EDUCATION COMMITTEE

INDIA
Land, Life and Culture

History and Government

ROSEMARY SACHDEV

MACMILLAN LIBRARY

First published in 2009 by
MACMILLAN EDUCATION AUSTRALIA PTY LTD
15–19 Claremont Street, South Yarra 3141

Visit our website at www.macmillan.com.au or go directly to www.macmillanlibrary.com.au

Associated companies and representatives throughout the world.

National Library of Australia Cataloguing-in-Publication data

Sachdev, Rosemary.
    History and government / Rosemary Sachdev.

    ISBN 978 1 4202 6711 2
    Sachdev, Rosemary. India: Land, life and culture.
    Includes index.
    For primary school age.
    India – History – Juvenile literature. India – Politics and government – Juvenile literature.

954

Edited by Kath Kovac
Text and cover design by Peter Shaw
Page layout by Kerri Wilson
Photo research by Lesya Bryndzia
Illustrations by Damien Demaj, DEMAP

Printed in China

Acknowledgements

Dedicated to Jasbir, who gave me India, and to Arkin, Amaya and Naira who belong and who will read these books some day.

With special thanks to the Archaeological Survey of India in New Delhi and Aurangabad for permission to take photographs in the Ajanta Caves with a camera and tripod, and thanks to the National Museum of India, Janpath, New Delhi for permission to photograph replicas in the Museum shop. Lastly, many thanks to La Boutique, Sunder Nagar, New Delhi, for the photograph of their joint family and their help in allowing us to photograph prints, paintings and artefacts from their collection.

With many thanks to all those who gave time for photographs and interviews, for lending their children to be photographed and for helping in the many ways they did and especial thanks to Jatinder, without whose tireless travel and wonderful photographs, these books would never have happened.

The author and the publisher are grateful to the following for permission to reproduce copyright material:

All photographs courtesy of Jatinder Marwaha except for:
Margaret Bourke-White/Time & Life Pictures/Getty Images, **17** (top); La Boutique, New Delhi, **12** (top); National Museum Shop, **6** (top, middle), **7** (bottom); PIB, Government of India, **19** (right); Collection of RJ Sachdev, **3** (left), **5** (top), **7** (top), **8** (right), **10** (all), **12** (bottom), **13** (all), **14** (all), **15** (top), **16**, **20**, **30** (top); RJ Sachdev, **17** (top), **23** (top).

While every care has been taken to trace and acknowledge copyright, the publisher tenders their apologies for any accidental infringement where copyright has proved untraceable. Where the attempt has been unsuccessful, the publisher welcomes information that would redress the situation.

Contents

Showing respect

Indian people always use titles with people's names to be polite, such as Shri and Shrimati if speaking Hindi, the national language, or Mr and Mrs if speaking English. These titles are different all over India, and their form depends on the family relationship or the seniority of the person addressed.

Glossary Words

When a word is printed in **bold**, you can look up its meaning in the Glossary on page 31.

India, a land of diversity

India is a land of great **diversity**, which can be seen in its arts, culture, people, landscape and climates. For every description of Indian life, there are many different but equally true variations.

India has a very long history. People have lived in India for around 10 000 years and come from many different racial backgrounds. They speak hundreds of languages; some spoken by millions of Indians, others spoken by only a few thousand. The country has many different landscapes and climates, from freezing mountains to hot, tropical areas.

India came under British influence in the 1600s, and Britain took control of India in the 1850s. India gained its independence from Britain in 1947 and became a **republic** in 1950.

Ancient carvings

Mountainous landscapes

Majestic tombs

Many religions

Unique plants

Wild animals

This book looks at India's long history. It explores its ancient civilisations, British rule and occupation, the formation of India's government, and the development of India as a nation.

History and government

India has a very long history of about 10 000 years, and has been governed by different people at different times. It is now the world's largest democracy, with more than a billion people.

Early kingdoms

Hundreds of years ago, India was broken into many kingdoms, each with its own ruler. The Hindu rulers were called Rajas or Maharajas. Muslim invaders first came to India around 700 CE, but did not settle there until about 1200 CE. Muslims who ruled from Delhi were later called emperors, and Muslim rulers of smaller kingdoms were called Nawabs.

Ferrcy Sier.

The Muslim emperor Feruz Shah Tughlaq ruled large areas of India from Delhi in the 1300s.

The British in India

In the 1600s, the British East India Company arrived to trade with India. They stayed for many years, and gained control of many parts of India. The company made treaties with various rulers and gradually took over their territories. By the mid-1800s, the company was the main political and military power in India. Its rule, however, ended in 1858 following a rebellion in 1857. The British government took control of the country. However, some Maharajas and Nawabs still ruled their own states, partly under British control, until 1947.

Did You Know?

India is named after the Indus River.

Independence

After using peaceful methods to make the British leave, India finally gained **independence** in 1947. Most of the state rulers joined India after Independence, but some joined Pakistan.

India's first cities were built around the Indus River, which starts in Tibet, then flows through India, but now flows mostly through Pakistan.

Early civilisations

India has 10 000-year-old **Stone Age** sites with rock shelters and rock paintings. Rock tools dating from the Stone Age have been found in many areas.

The Indus Valley Civilisation

The earliest known cities in India date from about 4500 years ago. These cities were built near the Indus River and were part of the Indus Valley Civilisation.

In the 1870s, people found bricks and bits of walls near the Indus River. In the 1920s, archaeologists found a whole city buried under mud and sand. The cities' houses were built of baked bricks. They had rooms around a courtyard with a well for water, and one door opened to the street. The people wore wool and cotton cloth and made many tools, jewellery, pottery, clay toys and stone images.

No one knows why the Indus Valley Civilisation ended. It may have been destroyed by floods, fires, earthquakes or invaders, or deserted as a result of a changing climate.

Indus Valley people made seals with figures of animals and writing. No one can read the writing today. Some seals have been found in west Asia, showing that the people traded with other regions.

This is a replica of a clay toy dating from 2500 BCE, found at an Indus Valley excavation site.

For Your Information

Many sites have been found since 1947 in north and west India, showing that the civilisation was larger than originally thought. It also extended into parts of Pakistan.

The cities of the Indus Valley Civilisation were well planned, with straight streets and underground drainage.

Early kingdoms

While the Indus Valley civilisation declined, new people came into India, possibly from central Asia. These people spoke languages from what is called the Indo-Aryan group.

The ancient Indians

These nomadic people were part of the first recorded migration into India, and started living around the Ganga River about 3500 years ago. They worshipped gods of nature and the fire god. They were cattle herders and used horses and carriages, and they soon settled into village life and grew rice, wheat and other cereals.

The ancient Indians composed the great Indian epics, which were long poems telling the stories of heroes of the Mahabharata and the Ramayana. Their priests, called Brahmins, knew the words and shared the stories with the people.

Excavations at Indraprastha in South Delhi unearthed the remains of buildings from more than 2000 years ago.

Contact between India and Greece led to a Greek influence on Indian art.

Alexander the Great

Greek ruler Alexander the Great tried to conquer India for its riches about 2300 years ago. However, he did not go beyond the Indus River, as most of his army wanted to go home. After eight years of fighting, they were exhausted and many fell sick. Some Greeks stayed behind and settled in India.

Early rulers

Emperor Ashoka was a famous Indian ruler who lived about 2300 years ago in the eastern area of India. He fought a great battle in eastern India in which thousands of people were killed. Ashoka was so horrified that he became a Buddhist, and had words of Buddhist **philosophy** carved on stone pillars and rocks across the country.

For Your Information

Some of the words that Ashoka carved included:
- People were to obey their parents, be liberal to friends and relatives and not kill animals
- All religious **sects** in the areas he ruled should live in peace
- People should show restraint of speech, which meant no praising of one's own faith or insulting other faiths.

Ashoka's edicts, which told people about himself as well as what they should do, were also carved on rocks across India. This replica of a rock from Gujarat stands outside the National Museum in Delhi.

Early languages and universities

The words Ashoka carved were in a language called Pali, which most people spoke. Sanskrit was only known to the priests. Universities were established in India more than 2000 years ago. They taught Buddhism, the Hindu scriptures, philosophy, logic and grammar.

Ashokan columns inscribed with Ashoka's edicts, or rules, were erected in many parts of India.

Southern kingdoms

South India had a number of famous kingdoms from 300 BCE to 700 CE that were ruled by different families. The kingdoms contained cities, towns, villages and ports. Most of south India is quite close to the sea, so many cities were on the coast.

Trade with other parts of India and other regions, combined with the rich, fertile land, made many of these kingdoms wealthy. However, many of the kingdoms fought each other. The larger kingdoms lasted a long time, but those with weak rulers were conquered.

South and central Indian culture

Much great literature was composed from 300 BCE to 700 CE and art and architecture were also important. Many wonderfully carved temples were built, and the Ajanta and Ellora caves were constructed by carving them from the solid rock face of hills.

The Ajanta Caves in central India contain many wall paintings and some sculptures.

This Hindu temple at Ellora was carved from the rock face of a hill.

Muslim rule and traders

Soon after 700 CE, Arabs arrived in the west of India. They destroyed some rich temples but also started trading. By the 1000s, more Muslims had come from Afghanistan and Turkey to trade or to steal India's riches. The first Muslim sultan, or king, settled in Delhi in about 1200.

Arrival of the Mughals

In 1526, a great **Mughal** warrior called Babar came to India from central Asia via Afghanistan and defeated the Muslim ruler in Delhi using cannons and archers on horses. He ruled over all of north India after defeating the local rulers, but returned to Afghanistan and died four years later.

Great Mughal buildings

The Mughal rulers after Babar built great buildings in Agra and Delhi. Akbar built the city of Fatehpur Sikri, outside Agra, and began building the Agra Fort. The fort was completed by his grandson, Shah Jahan, who built the Taj Mahal in Agra and the walled city of Delhi, including the Red Fort.

For Your Information

Shah Jahan built the Taj Mahal as a tomb for his wife, who died after having their fourteenth child. In 1666, he was buried in the same tomb.

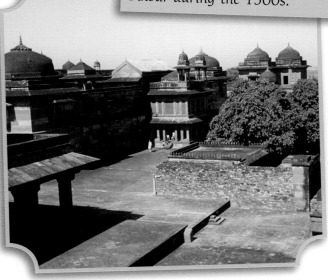

Many tourists visit the deserted city of Fatehpur Sikri, built by Akbar during the 1500s.

The Agra Red Fort was built as a royal residence and the administrative centre of the government.

Decline of Mughal rule

The last great Mughal ruler, Aurangzeb, died in 1707. The Mughal rulers that came after him ruled for another 150 years, but they were all weak. Strong men in different parts of India broke away from the Mughal empire and set up their own kingdoms.

European and British traders

During the reign of the Mughals, all the European countries wanted to trade with India. The major trade was in spices, especially pepper. The French, the Dutch, the Danes and the British signed trade agreements with the Mughal emperors and other rulers and built trading settlements near the sea.

The earliest British East India Company building that still exists is in Chennai, previously called Madras.

MEET Professor Nalini Thakur

Professor Nalini Thakur is an architectural **conservationist** and a qualified architect. She studied building conservation in Italy and England, and has done conservation work all over India.

In conversation with Professor Nalini Thakur

I became interested in history and the need for saving neglected historical buildings while studying architecture in Delhi. I've worked on buildings in places such as Hampi, Khajuraho, Brindaban and Champaner, which was declared a **world heritage site**.

British rule and colonisation

After the decline of the Mughal rulers, new people, such as the rulers of Hyderabad and Oudh, came to power in different parts of India. They had earlier been appointed by the Mughals to control these areas. The British did not want any powerful kingdoms in India, so they sent in armies to try to defeat them. Some of the soldiers were British, but most of them were Indian. India was a divided country.

Marathas and Sikhs

In western India, the Marathas gained control over areas once ruled by the Mughals. In the north, the Sikhs built their own kingdom. The British fought wars to defeat these large independent kingdoms. With other rulers, the British signed treaties to ensure that they behaved as the British wanted.

Annexation of India's kingdoms

Some of India's British rulers had good ideas for the country, but their main purpose was to gain more land and control for Britain. If the British decided a ruler was not doing a good job, they took over and sent the ruler away into exile in another part of India.

These toy soldiers from the 1800s show Indian men dressed in British military uniforms.

The British took control of the city of Lucknow in 1856, claiming the Muslim ruler was not ruling properly.

British changes to India

The British brought the railways to India, which helped British trade. They also wanted Indians to become Christians. This upset the Indian people, and was one of the reasons for a big **revolt** in the north in 1857.

For Your Information

The British discouraged Indian crafts, especially the weaving of cloth. Indians were forced to plant more cotton, which was sent to Britain, made into cheap cloth in British factories, and sold back to India at a high price. The **handloom** industry suffered greatly.

This siege train, with weapons and men, reached Delhi in 1857 to try and regain control of the city from the Indians who had revolted against the British.

When the last Mughal ruler was sent into exile in Burma in 1858, the British Government took complete control of India from the British East India Company.

Indian reformers

In the 1800s, a number of Indians wanted to reform some old, bad Indian practices. Ram Mohan Roy wanted to combine the best of Indian culture with the best of western ideas and science, and started a new society called the Brahmo Samaj based on this idea.

Very young girls were often married to older men. If their husbands died and the girls became widows, they had to leave the family and beg for a living. Ishwar Chandra Vidyasagar organised the remarriage of widows, tried to stop child marriages and started schools for girls.

Bombay University was founded in 1857, at the same time as Calcutta University. The decision was made to teach Indians English so the Empire could employ English-speaking Indians in the British capital Calcutta.

British ruling policy

India had always been a land of many rulers, with states of different sizes. When the British took control of India, they allowed many of these state rulers to stay, but under a British 'Resident' who actually controlled the ruler. Much of India was ruled directly by the British.

Nationalism

When the railways came to India, people could move around more easily and learn more about their country. Following the work and teaching of a number of educated Indians, Indian people realised that the British were foreigners who were only concerned about their own country. Indians started seeing themselves as belonging to all of India, and they wanted the British to leave.

In 1885, the Indian National Congress was started by a British man, A.O. Hume, to allow Indians to discuss the problems they had with the British.

For Your Information

After the 1857 revolt, many of the British came to despise Indians. They complained about Indian customs without trying to understand them. There was almost no social interaction between the British and the Indian people. The British widely considered Indians as inferior people, fit only to be servants and low-ranking soldiers.

British people had their meals cooked by Indian kitchen servants.

The British hired Indians as servants to help them dress, carry their belongings and pull fans to keep them cool.

Mahatma Gandhi

Mahatma Gandhi was a lawyer who had studied in England and returned to India in 1915. He started a peaceful movement that he hoped would make the British leave India. Mahatma Gandhi asked all his followers to practise **civil disobedience**, and non-cooperation with the government, but only while following Satyagraha, which means using truth and non-violence to overcome injustice.

महात्मा गांधी
MAHATMA GANDHI

These stamps show Mahatma Gandhi as a young and old man.

Many people followed Mahatma Ghandi and did what he asked. They also burned their British clothes and wore clothes made of khadi, a rough, hand-spun and hand-woven cotton cloth. Mahatma Gandhi learned to spin cotton to make khadi cloth and encouraged his followers to learn as well. Khadi is rough, but the people were happy to defy the British who could not stop them from wearing these clothes.

MEET Shri Devi Prasad

Shri Devi Prasad trained as a painter at art school and became interested in the philosophy of Mahatma Gandhi. In 1944, he started work as an art instructor at Mahatma Gandhi's Sewagram **ashram** and stayed for 18 years. He is sad that people today have a desire for **materialism** and status, which have no place in Gandhian philosophy.

In conversation with Shri Devi Prasad

I am an optimist and I hope people will give up materialism. Otherwise, they may destroy themselves.

Independence and Partition

After many years of peaceful struggle, the British decided they could no longer rule India. World War II had just finished, and it had exhausted Britain and left it very poor. The British left India in 1947, but before they left, they **partitioned** it into two different countries.

India's first prime minister

Pandit Nehru, like Mahatma Ghandi, was a lawyer who had studied in Britain. He came from a very wealthy family, but gave up everything when he joined Mahatma Gandhi's movement of civil disobedience. He wore khadi and learned how to spin cotton thread on a hand spinning wheel. Pandit Nehru was jailed many times by the British and wrote several great books during his years of imprisonment.

Pandit Nehru became the first prime minister of independent India. He gave a famous speech at midnight just before Independence: 'At the stroke of the midnight hour, when the world sleeps, India will awake to life and freedom.'

This stamp was issued just after Pandit Nehru's death in 1964 and shows him in his familiar 'Gandhi' cap and with the rose he always wore in his coat after Independence.

Partition

Before Independence, many Muslims felt that a free India would become a Hindu country, and they demanded a separate country for themselves. Mahatma Gandhi and Pandit Nehru were against this, but Muslim leaders started **agitating**. The British divided India into two. This was called Partition.

Did You Know?

Mahatma Gandhi was shot and killed less than a year after Partition by a Hindu **fanatic**, because Mahatma Gandhi wanted friendship between Pakistan and India.

When the state of Punjab was divided in two, more than 14 million Hindus, Sikhs and Muslims fled between the Indian and Pakistani sides of the new border.

India becomes two countries

In 1947, Pakistan was carved out of India in two parts, East Pakistan and West Pakistan. These were areas where there were more Muslims than Hindus. East Pakistan became an independent country called Bangladesh in 1971.

MEET Sadarni Kirpal Kaur and Sadarni Avtar Kaur

Sadarni Kirpal Kaur was a teacher living in Lahore in 1947. Kirpal Kaur and her sister Avtar Kaur listened to Pandit Nehru make his famous Independence speech at Kirpal Kaur's school. Two days later, they left Pakistan for ever. Kirpal Kaur, 93, (right) now lives in Delhi and Avtar Kaur, 86, (left) lives in Canada.

In conversation with Sadarnis Kirpal Kaur and Avtar Kaur

Kirpal Kaur: We were in tears because of the riots but were so proud that we were a free country at last.

Avtar Kaur: We were freedom fighters in college. We attended rallies and wore clothes of khadi cloth.

Dominion and republic

On 15 August 1947, India became independent with Dominion status. India adopted a new flag and a new national anthem based on a poem by the **Nobel Laureate** Rabindranath Tagore.

Reorganisation of India's states

India's states now had to be reorganised to include the 510 semi-independent **princely states** that had decided to join free India. Some of the states were very small, and some were very large and wealthy. As the former British India and the princely states had become one country, the new Indian Government realised that the state boundaries would have to change.

India's new national flag was unfurled at midnight before the day of 15 August 1947.

Key

Princely states

Ruled by Britain

BRITISH INDIA

The boundaries and names shown on this map do not imply official endorsement and may not be correct.

For Your Information

The new flag was a tricolour with three horizontal stripes of saffron, white and green. The flag shows a wheel from an Ashokan sculpture in the centre, emphasising the length of India's history.

This map of pre-independence India from 1947 shows British India and the area ruled by 554 princely states.

Republic Day

On 26 January 1950, India declared itself a republic. India had written a new **constitution** and a president was elected. After this date, Britain had no further role in India.

A new national emblem was also chosen at this time. It was adapted from a sculpture of four lions with the words 'Truth Alone Triumphs' written in Sanskrit along the bottom.

Later changes to state boundaries

Changes were made to the state boundaries in 1956, so that people who spoke the same main language belonged to one state. These changes are still happening. Some large states have been divided to make smaller states that are more easily governed, and some new states have been formed because of the different languages spoken.

Union territories

Some small areas of India, called union territories, are ruled directly by the Central Government. Two of these are the two island groups to the west and east of India.

Republic Day is celebrated with a grand parade every year.

India's national emblem was taken from a sculpture from the time of the Emperor Ashoka.

The government

India has a Central Government as well as state governments. The Central Government has two houses: the Lok Sabha, or the people's house, and the Rajya Sabha, or the council of states. The larger state governments may have one or two houses, called state assemblies.

The Lok Sabha

Members of the Lok Sabha are elected directly by the people in national elections. Their term of office is five years. The Speaker of the Lok Sabha controls the functioning of the Lok Sabha and is elected from its members.

The Rajya Sabha

Members of the Rajya Sabha are elected by members of the Lok Sabha and the state assemblies. The term of each Rajya Sabha as a whole is six years, but one third of the members retire every two years and an equal number is elected at this time.

The prime minister

The prime minister of India is chosen by the largest political party in the Lok Sabha. He or she then chooses a Council of Ministers. The Council's decisions must be approved by both Houses of Parliament before they become law.

India's Parliament House, called Sansad Bhavan, is in New Delhi.

The Indian Government

The Indian Government has three main organisations. The Legislature consists of the elected members of parliament who make laws. The Administration is made up of government employees who carry out the work. The Judiciary are the judges who decide whether the laws are being followed.

Elections

All Indians over 18 years of age are eligible to vote, although voting is not compulsory. Although India now uses electronic voting machines, elections take many weeks as the machines have to be taken up mountains and into jungles to allow all the millions of Indians to vote. As many people could not read at the time of Independence, political parties use symbols instead of written names during elections.

Village councils

Each village has a council called a Panchayat, which is the basic unit of democracy in India. In 2008, there were nearly 240 000 panchayats, with 2 600 000 elected members, of which 1 000 000 were women.

For Your Information

Panchayatraj, the government of the council, is a very old system where five village elders make decisions for the village. 'Panch' means five and 'raj' means government.

Village councils, called Panchayats, are elected by the village for five years.

MEET Agnelo D'Souza

Agnelo D'Souza is the Sarpanch, or chief, of the Arpora village panchayat in Goa.

In conversation with Agnelo D'Souza

We try and solve people's problems and receive proposals for development work such as roads, drains and lighting. We have fortnightly meetings. We now have one new female member and two new young members. I have been a member for 15 years and Sarpanch three times.

After Independence

At Independence, India was a land with many very poor people. Eighty per cent of the population lived in villages and had very little education. There were not enough roads, houses, schools or hospitals, and little clean water or electricity.

Socialism

The first Prime Minister of India, Pandit Nehru, believed strongly in socialism. Socialism is a political movement in which the Government looks after the people, providing housing, education and healthcare.

Under socialism, India made just two types of cars: a Morris, called an Ambassador, and a Fiat, shown here.

All major projects, such as dams for water, electricity supply and steel plants, were developed by the socialist government.

Problems for India

By the end of the 1950s, India had used up the **foreign exchange** that it had owned at Independence. The country could no longer afford to import anything, except essentials such as rice, wheat and oil. Indian factories had only just started making goods that were once imported, so life was very hard.

Bad droughts in the 1960s made food scarce. Wheat, rice and sugar could only be bought with ration cards, and the amount rationed was just enough for a family.

For Your Information

India fought three wars with Pakistan after Independence. India also fought against China, who invaded the far north-east of India in 1962.

Nationalisation

In the 1970s, Prime Minister Indira Gandhi easily won the election, using the slogan of 'Banish poverty'. She decided that the government should take over all the large private banks, insurance companies and coal mines. This was called nationalisation.

The Green Revolution

With irrigation, better crop seeds and fertilisers, India grew enough food to feed all its people for the first time. This became known as the 'Green Revolution'. India can now export grains and can donate food to countries during **famines** or wars.

Wheat harvests improved greatly in the 1970s.

The White Revolution

Milk products were produced under a co-operative scheme called Amul that had orginally started in the 1940s. During the 1970s, Amul expanded in what became known as the 'White Revolution'. Small farmers with one or two cows gave milk to the cooperative and were paid good prices. This made their lives easier, and meant India had enough milk for everyone.

Did You Know?

India is the largest producer of milk products in the world.

Amul makes milk powder, baby milk, butter, cheese, yoghurt, ice cream, chocolate and every other milk product.

Economic changes

By the 1980s, many of the factories that the government had taken over under nationalisation were doing very badly. The people running the factories had no real interest in making a profit. The government paid their salaries even if the factory was running at a loss and employees still received their salaries even if the factories closed down.

In Mumbai, many textile factories have closed due to competition from synthetic fabrics and the high value of land.

Delayed projects

Many of the major projects designed by the Government took a long time to build. Because of delays, the costs increased. There was still a great shortage of electricity and water in the cities, but new projects were slow to be developed.

Financial problems

By 1990, India had no foreign money left, even to import necessary goods. Finance Minister S. Manmohan Singh, who was an **economist**, decided to open the economy and allow goods to be imported. He encouraged foreign people to invest in India.

24

Privatisation and foreign investment

Under privatisation, many of the government-run organisations, such as banks and insurance companies, became public companies and sold shares to the people. They are now making a profit. Many factories were sold to private people who could run them efficiently. Foreign competition was allowed, so companies had to be professionally run.

Labour costs are very low in India, compared with countries in the western world. It is very profitable for other countries to set up factories in India and use Indian labour.

Mobile phone towers are located all through India and almost everyone can now afford a mobile phone, so people in cities can call their families in the villages.

Many different cars are now manufactured in India, and private airlines have started operating.

For Your Information

The railways are still fully controlled by the government, and they are very important for the many poor people of India. Many new, fast, comfortable trains have been introduced, and at present they are well managed and making a profit.

MEET Professor Sudhir Shah

Professor Sudhir Shah studied in Delhi and America and is now a professor at the Delhi School of Economics at the University of Delhi. He has taught in Cincinatti and has been an examiner in Holland and Singapore. He is happier working in India, which he feels has a better intellectual environment.

In conversation with Professor Sudhir Shah

It's an exciting time in India as it is going through a big transition. When I left India, it was a depressed economy. It was always 'jam yesterday, jam tomorrow, but never jam today'.

The media

Newspapers report what is happening throughout India and the world. As almost all educated Indians read English, the English-language newspapers are very popular. Radio and television broadcasts are also available across the country.

Indian newspapers

About 60 different English-language newspapers are available, as well as many in each regional language. Major cities have their own editions of the same paper. Major English papers are *The Hindustan Times*, *The Times of India* and *The Indian Express*. Many of the papers have one or more Indian-language editions as well.

Newspapers are available in every major Indian language and many of the minor ones.

News magazines

Weekly news magazines are very popular and include discussions on matters concerning India's people. They are published in English, Hindi and regional languages.

English magazines can be bought or delivered for the cost of a subscription.

Radio and television

Until 1991, Indian radio and television were controlled by the government. Only one radio station, called All India Radio, was available. It broadcast government news, educational programs and classical music. The government Doordarshan channel was the only television channel.

Television came to India in the 1960s. Programs were only broadcast for a short time each day. Colour television was first available during the 1982 Asian Games. Most of the television news was in pure Hindi, which few people could understand, but a short English news bulletin was also given.

Cable and satellite television

With the arrival of cable television, the Indian Government changed its programming policies. Many private channels and discussion programs are now telecast in both English and commonly spoken Hindi. India also has satellite television. A small satellite dish allows many programs to be shown in all languages.

Did You Know?

One satellite television provider has 21 news and knowledge channels in Hindi and English, eight sports channels, nine children's channels and many more in regional languages.

Satellite television programs come from all parts of the world.

the IT revolution

It has been easy for India to become the world hub of information technology (IT), because India has such a large English-speaking population. Some of the major IT world players are Indians, whether based in or out of India. The IT revolution has also led to the growth of cities, especially in south India.

Indians adapted to computer technology very early. Government and private offices all use computers, although some government work is still being transferred to computers.

Infosys provides consultancy, engineering and IT services at their campus in Bangalore.

IT businesses

A number of IT firms started by Indians are listed on world stock exchanges, and IT business parks have been established, mostly in south India. Two of the organisations based in Bangalore are Infosys and Wipro. Indians have created computer software for organisations all over the world.

For Your Information

Many young Indians are hired as call centre operators to answer questions from countries such as Australia and America. Because of the time differences, Indians work in offices that function all night. They answer calls, check their computers and pass on the information to the overseas caller.

Many towns have IT centres where young people can learn computer skills, and all Indian towns have Internet cafés.

Growth of cities

According to the 2001 **census**, India had three major cities with between 13 and 16 million people each: Delhi, Kolkata and Mumbai. As the population is increasing all the time, these figures are no longer accurate. The next census will be held in 2011.

Ahmedabad, Bangalore, Chennai and Hyderabad are smaller cities that each have more than five million people. The rapid population increase in the last three cities is due to the IT revolution.

Many Indian cities now have malls with western-style shops, but most people still shop at the local general stores.

MEET Asgar Ali

Asgar Ali has been the shopkeeper of a general store outside Udaipur in Rajasthan since 1970. He opens the shop from 7.00 a.m. to 9.00 p.m.

In conversation with Asgar Ali

My shop is for ordinary people. I sell grains such as flour and rice, lentils, tea, spices and general household goods. Everyone knows they can get decent stuff and good prices from me.

The future

India has a very bright future as many Indians are trained in using different forms of technology and there are many good jobs. Indians have always had a great interest in astronomy and, in 2008, launched 10 satellites from one rocket. India also sent a lunar probe to the Moon in October 2008.

Did You Know?

The Maharaja of Jaipur, Sawai Jai Singh, built five observatories in India in the 1700s.

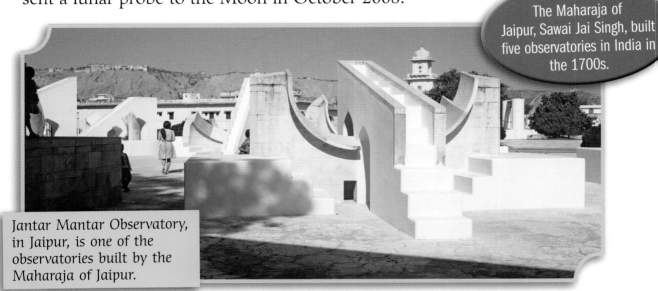

Jantar Mantar Observatory, in Jaipur, is one of the observatories built by the Maharaja of Jaipur.

Jobs in India

Many young people left India, believing there was no decent future for them. Now, good jobs are available, so they are returning. Their salaries may not be as high, but living expenses are lower. Many women are now well educated and can work full time.

For Your Information

Family ties in India are still very close. The country has a very strong pull on Indians, who will always come back for a family celebration or at any other opportunity.

MEET Professor U.R. Rao

Professor U.R. Rao is the foremost Indian space scientist. He is responsible for helping to develop India's advanced space exploration and satellite program.

In conversation with Professor U.R. Rao

Indian satellites are among the best in the world for communications and remote sensing. We are now venturing into interplanetary exploration as the future beckons us.

Glossary

agitating	causing public unrest to raise awareness of a controversial issue
ashram	a place where people can seek refuge from the world and meditate
censored	stopped publication of reports in newspapers to protect the government
census	official count of a country's population
civil disobedience	to refuse to obey government laws that are seen as unfair
conservationist	someone who protects buildings of historical importance
constitution	the written principles by which a country is governed
diversity	great variety
economist	an expert in economics or the management of finances
fanatic	a person who has extreme ideas and acts on them
famines	very bad shortages of food or water in a district
foreign exchange	the money of another country
handloom	a hand-operated loom for weaving cloth
independence	free from the control of a foreign country
materialism	belief that only objects and belongings are important in life
Mughal	Muslim rulers of India in the 1500s
Nobel Laureate	winner of a Nobel Prize in peace, literature or science
partitioned	separated into more than one country
philosophy	an attempt to understand life and the human mind
princely states	areas of India governed by independent rulers until 1947
republic	a form of government where the rulers are elected by the people and the leader is usually called the President
revolt	a rebellion against authority, in this case a foreign power
sects	different divisions within a religion
Stone Age	the period in history when tools were made only of stone
world heritage site	a place decided by UNESCO as being of outstanding value to the world

Index